Christian roots, contemporary spirituality

Christian roots, contemporary spirituality

Lynda Barley

Church House Publishing
Church House
Great Smith Street
London SW1P 3NZ

Tel: 020 7898 1451
Fax: 020 7898 1449

ISBN-13 978-0-7151-4102-1
ISBN-10 0 7151 4102 3

Published 2006 by Church House Publishing.

Copyright © The Archbishops' Council 2006.

All rights reserved. No part of this publication may be reproduced or stored or transmitted by any means or in any form, electronic or mechanical, including photocopying, recording, or any information storage and retrieval system without written permission which should be sought from the Copyright Administrator, Church House Publishing, Church House, Great Smith Street, London SW1P 3NZ

Email: copyright@c-of-e.org.uk

The opinions expressed in this book are those of the author and do not necessarily reflect the official policy of the General Synod or The Archbishops' Council of the Church of England.

Printed in England by Halstan & Co. Ltd, Amersham, Bucks

Contents

Foreword vi

Series introduction vii

Introduction xi

1. **Listening to the nation** 1
   We believe in . . . 1
   Modern spirituality 6
   i Generation 10
   Christian traditions 12
   Secularization 16

2. **Listening to the local** 19
   Back to church 19
   Christmas longings 21
   Christmas roots 23
   Remembering 26
   Family occasions 28

3. **Listening to the past** 33
   Public faith 33
   Believing without belonging 36
   Religious capital 37
   Our inheritance 39

4. **Surprising signs of the times** 40
   Prayer and authentic spirituality 41
   Christmas 47
   Family specials 50
   Towards a future 53

Notes 54

Foreword

We live in an ever-changing and increasingly fragmented society where the role of local churches is becoming more and more diverse. The challenge for churches to make the gospel fresh for every generation is specially vivid just now. As our nation and society become increasingly complex it is important to understand the languages of belief being spoken. The significant contributions churches make to individual lives, communities and wider society are often not fully understood either by those inside or by those outside the institution. Good research can help us properly reflect on the place we find ourselves. Evidence-based research is an accepted part of modern life and the dialogue it creates can powerfully help local churches consider before God their place in his mission to today's world.

+ Rowan CANTUAR:

Series introduction

A changing Church

> The Church of England is only beginning to grasp the scale of the social and cultural changes that have transformed its missionary context in recent years. British culture has changed and perceptions and expectations of Christianity and of the Church have changed with it.

These are the words of Bishop Graham Cray, introducing the recent book, *Evangelism in a Spiritual Age*.[1] The Church's conversation with our country must respond to this challenge and be prepared to adapt. For too long it has been one-sided, the Church imagining people as it would like them to be, rather than listening to where they are. Father Vincent Donovan, in his classic book, *Christianity Rediscovered*,[2] described his attempts to introduce Christianity to the Masai people in East Africa and spoke of the necessity of bringing the gospel to where people are. He pictures a church without uniformity, specialization and centralization and asks how the church should respond to culture and so find new life in God. The consequences of such a conversational approach for outreach and mission are highly significant. Pope John Paul II suggested that relating Christ to culture should be at the heart of evangelism. Yet, he observed that today 'countries with a Christian tradition are experiencing a serious rift between the gospel message and large areas of their culture'.[3]

In this series of research-based booklets, we shall be listening and seeking to discern the voices emanating from the shifting culture in which the churches find themselves witnessing to Christ in the world today. At the beginning of the twenty-first century in Britain, where do churches alter their mission methods to the changing modern-day culture and where do they stand apart? It was John Taylor, a former

Bishop of Winchester, who wrote that mission is about finding out what God is doing and then joining in[4] and the present Archbishop of Canterbury has picked up this and made it a focus in our day. Sheffield diocesan missioner, Sue Hope (writing in The *Vicar's Guide*[5]) adds: 'Learning how to interpret the Spirit, spotting the footprints of God in the earthiness of the ordinary life of a local community and following them into the unknown is at the heart of true mission'.

In various ways the religious tide in Europe has been changing radically since the Second World War. Successive governments have, for years, been persuaded by religious sociologists that secularization was taking over. They are now recognizing the reality of a postmodern, religiously pluralist society where faith groups play an important role in community life. Christian churches remain a major feature in national life but the culture around them is fast-moving and diverse. 'A plural, post-modern, fragmented world – a sackful of conflicting world views – presents a huge challenge.'[6] If Christian mission is to mean anything in modern Britain, churches must learn from the example of the apostle Paul, who listened to the cosmopolitan society in the Athens of his day and responded to its challenge.

In western society, people have been said to 'listen with their eyes and think with their feelings' and much professional advice towards improving modern-day relationships is given on this premise. Listening skills have never been more vital to church life but we must listen not just to what people say, but to what they feel, what they show and what they do. Listening with discernment to people today, to their lives and their stories is the purpose of these research booklets. It is not too late for our churches to take time to listen, to be prepared to learn and to adapt to the messages they hear.

The recent report, *Mission-shaped Church*,[7] has struck a chord with many who feel the Church should be more responsive to the spiritual needs of those with no experience of church and those who have drifted away. Fresh expressions of church are being planted successfully

Series introduction

across our land for young and old alike – some in unusual places. At the beginning of the twenty-first century, the *missio dei*, the mission of God, is guiding and leading us into particular new things while reminding us of the reassurance in the best of the traditional.

Opportunities in recent years to share some modern social and religious research findings have often been greeted with the encouraging response, 'So we need to reshape and revisit the basics'. The basics of our faith remain as relevant for our modern-day society as they ever were but the presentation and practice must change as society has changed. We need to regain our confidence in the spiritual and pastoral basics we offer a country that, in its turn, has lost its way.

WE NEED TO REGAIN OUR CONFIDENCE IN THE SPIRITUAL AND PASTORAL BASICS WE OFFER A COUNTRY THAT, IN ITS TURN, HAS LOST ITS WAY.

The road map for local churches today is fast-changing, diverse and rather bumpy. The Revd Andrew Cunnington recently wrote in his local parish magazine:

> Our church is changing and I feel as if we have the opportunity to be more like the church God intended – certainly more biblical in our character. We also have the opportunity to get weighed down and sunk without trace if we choose . . . Preoccupied by not enough money in the bank and not enough people in the pews and not enough people to get all the jobs done properly – that will sink us.

Many are beginning to feel that this is the modern-day challenge of God's Spirit to the churches in Britain.

Whether your church is a Rolls Royce model, a nippy Aston Martin, a family Ford saloon or a trusty transit van, my prayer is that the modern-day research messages brought together in this series will encourage you to take time to listen as God seeks to guide his Church along new paths. In recent years the importance of listening has come to the fore. Research could be said to be simply a systematic exercise

Christian roots, contemporary spirituality

in listening. When we listen and reflect on what we hear, we discover surprises that both encourage and challenge. Good, effective research helps us to listen to what the Spirit is saying to the churches (Revelation 2 and 3), to look up to where God is evident in the world and behold his glory.

Lynda Barley
Church House, Westminster

Introduction

Christian Britain is a thing of the past and yet it remains an inescapable backdrop to everyday life. In this short booklet I shall be exploring what this inherited faith still means in modern Britain, how it affects both personal lives and the community. We shall reflect on modern-day public faith and how it is developing amidst the international marketplace. In the initial chapters, 'Listening to the nation' and 'Listening to the local', the reader will discover common threads that need to be interpreted against the background of 'Listening to the past'. So, in the chapter of this title we explore the changing fortunes of religious practice over the past generation or so.

Pulling together these findings reveals some surprises! Being open to the research evidence yields both encouragements and challenges for local churches as they move into the twenty-first century. Several key surprises for churches to respond to are highlighted in the final chapter, 'Surprising signs of the times'. At first glance you may feel there is nothing new here; we may be getting back to basics but we are doing it in a fresh and relevant way for the twenty-first century. If our churches are to have a future, all who are concerned must continue to unwrap the surprises and follow the signposts. The examples shared in this chapter show how churches have responded to the 'Christian roots' research findings. They are intended to encourage you to continue to unwrap the research surprises explored in this booklet and to explore ways in which your church can build on the part of Christian Britain in which it finds itself. In our fragmented society it is even more important to 'scratch where people are itching' and this will involve each church responding to its inherited faith in a unique way. There are no definitive templates but signposts towards some surprising places in God's world today.

1

Listening to the nation

We believe in . . .

Religion in Britain is a private affair, almost a taboo subject for social conversation, even among close family and friends. Research conducted by David Hay and Ann Morisy in 1985[1] shows that we fear being thought stupid or mentally unbalanced if we talk about faith; responses that parallel those given in studies of social conformity. In 2000 David Hay and Kate Hunt[2] studied the spirituality of people who have no formal connection with a religious institution and never go to church. They found ample evidence of the presence of a spiritual life in everybody they talked with, but most people were timid when it came to talking about religion and nervous about mentioning it in public. They concluded 'that the perception of a hostile cultural environment is a major factor in keeping the religious feelings of many of our contemporaries "implicit".[3] Discerning religious views and affiliations is consequently an exercise in discovering hidden, even suppressed attitudes.

Over the years, researchers have struggled to categorize people's religious views in topic areas where the language used can be diverse and ambiguous. Surveys have depended on simple statements of faith in order more easily to record people's views and make general comparisons. Take, for example, belief in God. In spite of considerable forces of secularization, belief in God remains a majority view in Britain today. An international poll in 2004 by the independent opinion research company, ICM, revealed that 67% of the British population say they believe in God. Of course, it is impossible to know what people

Christian roots, contemporary spirituality

understand by belief in God in this context without further, more detailed research, but at least they are acknowledging an awareness of a supernatural force at work in the world. Britain has one of the lowest levels across the world of belief in God, in contrast with more than 80% recorded in most other countries, but it remains the consistent majority following, so countering claims of a secular society. As Alan Billings suggests, the British may lead secular lives but they still have sacred hearts.[4] The following graph shows how belief in God decreased particularly over the 1980s and 1990s and has slightly increased since the turn of the millennium.[5]

1. Belief in God (especially a personal god) **declining**

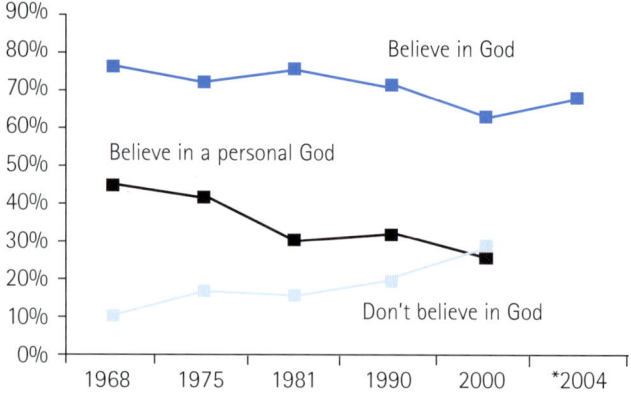

Q. Which, if any, of the following do you believe in? *(Gallup/ORB/ICM*)*

In 1968, over three-quarters (77%) of the population in Britain said they believed in God, whereas 35 years or so later, the proportion was 67%, just one in ten fewer. In contrast, 'belief in a personal God' declined more sharply – from 45% in 1968 to 26% in 2000 – a lower percentage than the proportion who did not believe in God. In 2000, three in ten people did not believe in God, almost a threefold increase from the level of one in ten (11%) recorded in 1968, nearly 40 years earlier. Results from other ongoing surveys by, for example, the National Centre for Social Research, ICM and MORI Ltd at the end of the twentieth century are in line with these figures.

Listening to the nation

Core Christian belief in a God may be declining slowly but some other traditional Christian beliefs have remained remarkably constant in the period from the 1960s to the 1990s.[6] Over half the population (52%) believe in heaven, over a quarter (28%) believe in hell, almost three-quarters (71%) believe in sin and nearly a third (32%) believe in the devil.[7] Of more interest is the increasing number who believe in a soul. Of course, this may be Godless, immortal and with little Christian association but belief in a soul has increased by 10% over the 1980s and 1990s when other traditional Christian beliefs were experiencing mixed fortune. In 2000 nearly seven in ten (69%) believed in a soul, while the less traditional belief in reincarnation only attracted the support of a quarter (25%), almost the same as in 1981 when a level of 27% was recorded. One recent national survey by MORI in 2003 for the BBC 1 *Heaven and Earth Show* is the first to indicate that belief in a soul may have become more widespread than belief in God.

BELIEF IN A SOUL MAY HAVE BECOME MORE WIDESPREAD THAN BELIEF IN GOD.

2. **Belief in a soul on the increase**

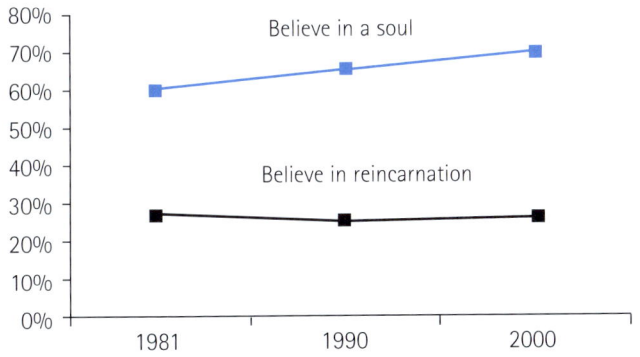

Q. Which, if any, of the following do you believe in? *(ORB 2000)*

Britons still believe in God; they increasingly believe in a soul and their sense of spiritual awareness is increasing. At the beginning of the twenty-first century, it is becoming more acceptable to admit to such awareness. Research for the BBC *Soul of Britain* programmes (2000)[8] revealed much greater awareness of personal spiritual experiences.

Christian roots, contemporary spirituality

Over three-quarters of people (76%) are now likely to admit to having had a religious or spiritual experience, compared to under half (48%) in 1987. Approaching four in ten (38%) have experienced an awareness of the presence of God, nearly the same proportion (37%) have experienced help in answer to prayer, while a quarter (25%) have experienced an awareness of the presence of evil, each of these proportions rising by over ten per cent across the previous thirteen years. A poll commissioned by Lloyds TSB in 2005 found that half of potential homebuyers now believe in ghosts.[9] Perhaps this resonates with the growing popularity of Hallowe'en but an estate agent of Knight Frank commented that the paranormal is a definite factor to consider when selling or buying a house. The national poll by MORI in 2003, in fact, found that 38% believed in ghosts and half of them had personal experience of them. The BBC research in 2000 also found that over half (55%) of adults recognize a transcendent providence – a patterning of events in a person's life that convinces them those events were meant to happen – compared to 29% in 1987. Compared to 16% in 1987, 29% have experienced an awareness of a sacred presence in nature.

3. **Spiritual awareness increasing as more people are aware of God, prayer and evil**

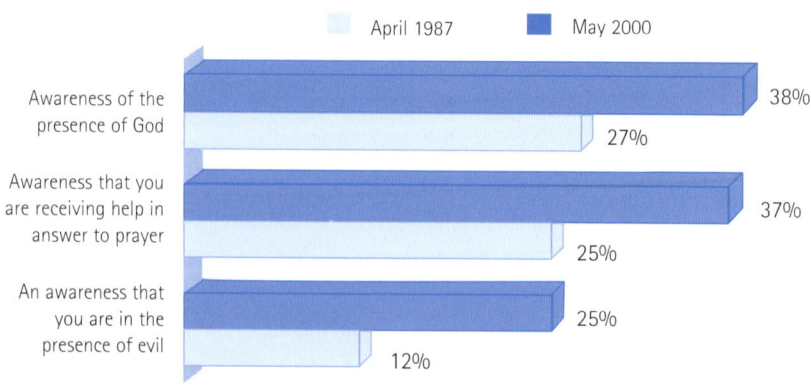

Q. People sometimes talk about certain kinds of personal experiences, which involve a non-everyday awareness of a presence or power. Have any of these happened to you? *(ORB 2000)*

But if spiritual awareness is increasing, it is not leading to increased religious affiliation. In the same national survey, over three in ten (31%) Britons admit to being 'a spiritual person' whereas slightly less (27%) admit to being 'a religious person'. In fact, over two in ten (21%) feel they are 'not a religious person' while just 7% feel they are 'not a spiritual person'. This leaves nearly a quarter (23%) expressing other views, a percentage matching the proportion reported as having no religious affiliation in the 2001 government census. Modern Britain embraces spirituality but sees no need to align itself with any formalized religion or faith community. Even membership of the British Humanist Association and the British National Secular Society only stand at 5,000 and 3,000 respectively.[10] Indeed, for many people today it is a Godless spirituality, a consumer-driven pick 'n' mix approach to spirituality or an inherited folk religion that is becoming acceptable, perhaps even fashionable. They see no need to conform to a single religious framework and no conflict in adopting belief systems according to individual preferences.

4. People see themselves as being more spiritual than religious

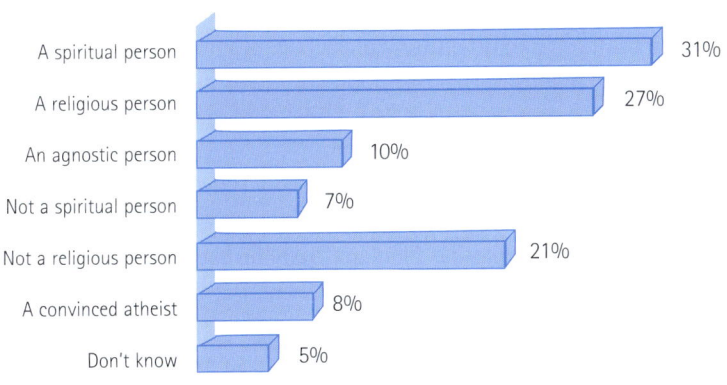

Q. Independently of whether you go to church or not, which of these would you say you are? *(ORB 2000)*

Christian roots, contemporary spirituality

Modern spirituality

In postmodern Britain many people are trying different forms of spirituality and religion. Theirs is the approach of modern-day consumer choice, pick 'n' mix experimentation with different aspects of various spirituality and faith traditions. It was David Beckham, the international footballer who, when asked whether he wanted his child baptized, famously replied 'Yes, but I'm not sure what religion.'[11] The widespread popularity of the Harry Potter fantasy fiction series by J. K. Rowling has been said to fill the God-shaped hole still in people's lives: 'The spirituality of Rowling is that of a muddled New Ager . . . [but it is] the spiritual search that has been a key of Harry's success.'[12] Reflecting this trend, in May/June 2005, Channel 4 showed a series of television programmes entitled *The Spiritual Shopper*. Participants were given four different spiritual practices for a month, to help re-energize and make them feel more positive. One participant experienced a Quaker prayer meeting, pagan drumming, Islamic prayer and t'ai chi.
In common with many spiritual searchers in the series, he wanted a spirituality that was easily accessible. To him, t'ai chi appeared the most easily attainable and was the practice he chose to continue. The range of spiritual groups in Britain today is growing fast but modern spirituality subtracts the off-putting aspects of religion and does not make difficult demands. It is a 'feel good' faith with the exotic experiential elements of various international religions.

Not many weeks before this, the BBC televised a series entitled *The Monastery* in which five young men spent 40 days and nights at Worth Abbey in West Sussex exploring their spiritual life. Each one left a changed person; one found a personal faith and the Church received many enquiries from non-churchgoers for retreats and opportunities for explorations of vocation. Dom Antony Sutch, subsequently commenting in the *Times*,[13] found a growing identity crisis among young men and the overriding need for stability in the lives of those 'who seek', these days. His piece explored the spiritual vacuum experienced by many men and their lack of spiritual vocabulary. It was entitled 'Why male spirituality hasn't got a prayer'.

Mind, body, spirit experiences are becoming a popular pursuit today. Horoscopes, lucky charms, ghosts and foretelling the future have attracted attention for generations[14] and it is far from clear whether these beliefs make any difference in the lives of the people who claim to hold them. Some of these practices were popular in New Testament times but the beginning of the twentieth century has seen a sudden growth in mind, body, spirit festivals, literature and therapy groups. Bookshops stock more and more books on the subject while the shelves for world religions are diminishing. There are aspects of religion that are attractive to modern spiritual shoppers, but most religions are known for their rules and conformity, perceived in today's world as negative and repressive.

MODERN SPIRITUALITY SUBTRACTS THE OFF-PUTTING ASPECTS OF RELIGION AND DOES NOT MAKE DIFFICULT DEMANDS.

The world-famous Taizé Christian community in Burgundy, France has promoted a holistic spirituality including meditative prayer. This particular contemplative approach has become popular especially among young people but it has not become widely integrated into mainstream church life. Perhaps it is surprising, then, that when Opinion Research Business polled adults in Britain in 2000[15] as to whether they had tried a range of spiritual experiences, it was prayer that emerged as the clear favourite. Although many people in the survey had tried a range of spiritual experiences, it was prayer that was most valued. Four in ten people (41%) had tried prayer and for a quarter (25%), it was rated as important in their lives. In terms of popularity, none of the other options offered came near.

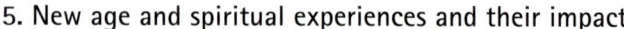

5. New age and spiritual experiences and their impact

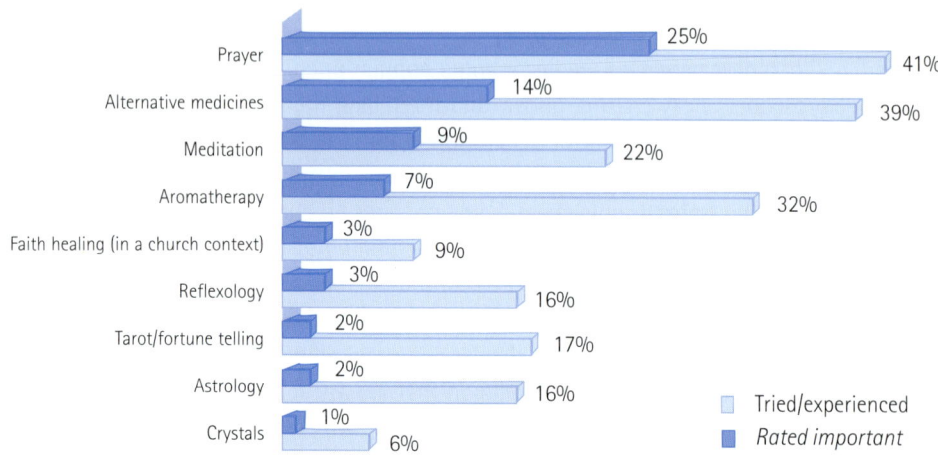

Qa. Which of the following have you tried or experiences?
Qb. And which are important in helping to live your life? *(ORB 2000)*

Prayer continues to be the most widely valued spiritual experience in modern-day Britain. When questioned by Populas in June 2005 for the *Sun*,[16] 65% of adults in Britain said they prayed. The British Social Attitudes survey in 1998 found that two-thirds (66%) of adults pray, over a third (38%) pray every month and a quarter (25%) every week. In 2001, Opinion Research Business found that a third of adults (33%) in Britain prayed at least once a week outside religious services and this included noticeably more women and older people. In fact, even among those who never attend church, 41% pray. A survey by the RAC Foundation in 2005 discovered that 73% of motorists said occasional prayers on the road, while 22% did so regularly. These prayers ranged from cries of help after passing a speed camera, to praying for those in need.

It is a sad reality that prayer and spirituality do not attract people towards religion and church attendance. Acknowledging the modern-day trend of de-secularization, Bishop Richard Chartres comments:

Listening to the nation

'We have to respect the fact that many spiritual people do not expect any great help from the church or believe that the Christian community is a fruitful place for searchers.'[17] A major piece of empirical research over 2000–2002, based on the area of Kendal in Cumbria, found that 'inner spirituality was present at the fringes of the congregational domain – in some Christian retreats centres and the Interfaith Group, for example – but nowhere at the heart of church life.'[18] This research into *The Spiritual Revolution*[19] discovered that the (declining) congregational domain was marked by a strong moralism and a focus towards God, along with, to varying extents, a concern with fellow humans and the individual self. This is at odds with the growing spiritual domain that was focused on the mind, body, spirit dimensions of life, being person-centred and concerned with inner wholeness.

One woman in her forties is described as summarizing her spiritual shift from the church thus:

> A one-hour service on Sunday? It's not really enough time to address your self-esteem issues, is it? I didn't find any help in the churches. I found it in a twelve step programme. That was the start of my personal journey.

What we are living through, the authors of *The Spiritual Revolution* maintain, is 'a period of unique change', 'a momentous shift in the sacred landscape'. But interestingly, they conclude that holistic spirituality will not take over from religion. It is practised mostly by middle-aged women, similar to many who attend congregations and, like religion, it has a limited appeal in its current form.

It is worth now turning our attention specifically to the younger generation, where this new research reveals insights that will challenge the way the Church relates to young people. The researchers found that there is, surprisingly, not much support for either Christian or New Age values among the younger generation, whom they describe as 'seeking without really finding'.[20] In this context it is interesting that in Sweden, philosophy cafés are becoming popular where the younger, seeking, 'non-atheistic' generation can discuss existential questions.[21] Perhaps in this unrestrained environment their explorations will include their grandparents' religions, of which they are largely ignorant.

iGeneration

In September 2004, the independent poll company, Populas, surveyed young adults in Britain between the ages of 18 and 30. The *Times* entitled the results the 'iGeneration Survey',[22] reflecting the individualist, self-centred, me, me, me approach of this generation and their reliance on electronic information technology. 'We are the iPod-loving children of Thatcher'. Only one in five (20%) is married, approaching a third (31%) have parents who are either separated or divorced, one in ten men work over 50 hours a week and more than a quarter have debts of at least £10,000 or more. The reports ran over several days, providing some memorable quotes:

> 'A hard working and savvy generation'
>
> 'We have no money but loads of stuff . . . We may be the first generation to be ruined by consumerism'.
>
> Here is 'the emergence of a new post-materialist value system, in which quality of life (has) assumed a greater value than material goods'.
>
> 'We still live like children . . . The "me" generation, the generation that never grew up'.

Listening to the nation

On matters of faith the iGeneration survey found some challenging results. Over half (52%) of young adults believe in life after death and 10% are willing to consider the possibility. Most believe that giving to charity is more important than voting. More than half have not attended a religious service outside the traditional rites of 'hatch, match and dispatch' since childhood, but 40% are members of a gym while 38% of men and 31% of women regularly work out in a gym.

> 'We put ourselves before our country and worship in gyms – not churches. We're fit and, my gosh, don't we know it.'
>
> 'The iGeneration still believes in ideals, such as justice, charity and an afterlife, but they don't believe in the "server" mechanisms traditionally used to arrange access to them.'
>
> 'Institutions like marriage, the Church, the police force and the legal system aren't enough to deliver or even guarantee any of these common ideals.'

OVER HALF (52%) OF YOUNG ADULTS BELIEVE IN LIFE AFTER DEATH AND 10% ARE WILLING TO CONSIDER THE POSSIBILITY.

The decline in Christian belief among the young is well documented.[23] The French sociologist, Yves Lambert, has commented that more and more young people who say they are religious or spiritual are anxious to add that they have no link with the Church.[24] For the iGeneration, belief is not matched by faith in institutions of the Church. The *Times* commented that this generation is 'willing to believe but its spiritual needs are not being met in church'. Many young people explore their spiritual thoughts and questions through pop music, yet 'the principal attitude towards secular popular culture among churches in the UK today has long been one of apathy and indifference . . . pop music is regarded as having become an alternative to religion, or even an alternative religion'.[25] There are pop artists who publicly profess a Christian faith, while many others increasingly deal specifically with religious themes in their music. 'A spiritual tsunami has hit postmodern culture', writes Leonard Sweet, 'this wave will build without breaking for decades to come. The wave is this: People want to know God.'[26] The *Times*, after several days of reflection on its own survey, concluded: 'The iGeneration is a dissatisfied one, and perhaps, a confused one . . . on the lookout for new ways to implement its ideals.'

Christian traditions

Not for the first time in history are the young searching for their own spiritual framework, but perhaps our global village has never before offered such a range of goods from which to choose. For its part, Britain today has many inherited Christian traditions to offer its citizens, but a visitor to this country would be forgiven for assuming that these are not particularly important to many. 'Laid-back Britain tolerates everything, except the state.' So ran the *Sunday Times* report following the 'World Values Survey'[27] in April 2005. Britain emerged as one of the most tolerant nations in the world, more accepting of alternative lifestyles, casual sex, divorce, drug use and different race neighbours, but less trusting of public institutions. Confidence in the political system in this country, for example, is half that in many other countries. Another international study, this time on behalf of the BBC World Service,[28] found that, worldwide, religious leaders are the most trusted leaders (by 33% of adults). They are followed by military/police leaders (26%), journalists (26%) and business leaders (19%) leaving politicians least trusted (13%). However, behind these global figures are wide variations between countries and regions with a low level of trust in all types of leader throughout Europe.

Much has been written about the British public's loss of confidence in institutions over recent years and the Church is not immune from this phenomenon. In 2000, Opinion Research Business[29] discovered that only 37% of the public had confidence in the Church as an institution. This was far less than levels of confidence attracted by the armed forces and the police – 76% and 64%, respectively – but more than Parliament, in which only 32% expressed confidence. Henley Centre research[30] shows that confidence in institutions picked up a little in the late 1990s after a steady decline across the 1980s and early 1990s but still the Church remained in the middle range. In very recent years child abuse cases and law and order developments both at home and abroad will have done little to improve public levels of confidence in individual institutions. The Church, along with other major institutions, has considerable ground to make up in this area.

MORI Social Research Institute approached this problem differently when it tracked levels of public confidence in certain professions.[31] In 1983 the most trusted occupations were clergymen/priests, doctors and teachers, while the least trusted were politicians, trade union officials and journalists. Twenty years later, doctors and teachers remain the most trusted occupations, politicians and journalists the least but clergy/priests have dropped 14% to fifth place and trade union officials have risen 15%.

Public confidence in the Church is about half the level of trust of that in its clergy and both have decreased significantly over the last 20 years. But all is not what it seems, in that the public has not discredited the traditions of the Church in the same way. Almost half (45%) the population regret the decline in traditional religion and think it makes Britain a worse country.[32] Church services of baptism, marriage and funerals continue to be valued to mark the traditional rites of passage through life. The numbers of such services may be declining but churchgoers and non-churchgoers continue to value their place in everyday life. Nearly eight out of ten (79%) adults in Britain feel it is important to hold a religious service to mark a death and over half (53%) feel it is important to mark a birth in this way. These proportions dropped over the decade leading up to the turn of the millennium but, as the graph below illustrates, most people want a religious service for the traditional hatch, match and dispatch.

If confidence in some of the church traditions remains, we have to ask why we are not seeing a greater take-up of the opportunities for Christian baptisms, marriages and funerals. Social pressures of conformity, together with local church pressures, must take much

Christian roots, contemporary spirituality

Whom do we trust?
Tell the truth

Occupations	1983	1993	2000	2003
Doctors	82%	84%	87%	91%
Teachers	79%	84%	85%	87%
Professors	n/a	70%	76%	74%
Judges	77%	68%	77%	72%
Clergy	85%	80%	78%	71%
Scientists	n/a	n/a	63%	65%
Police	61%	63%	60%	64%
Ordinary men/women	57%	64%	52%	53%
Civil servants	25%	37%	47%	46%
Trade Union officials	18%	32%	38%	33%
Business leaders	25%	32%	28%	28%
Politicians	18%	14%	20%	18%
Journalists	19%	10%	15%	18%

Q: Would you tell me if you generally trust them to tell the truth, or not?

Source: BMA/MORI   n/a = not available   Base: 2,141 British adults aged 15+

of the blame. The Church has foundations of faith that mean it cannot act as a spiritual supermarket where people make their own selections of belief. However, local churches need to reflect objectively on the particular hoops they impose and through which they expect prospective 'customers' to jump before they will conduct such services of Godly acceptance. Frequently, one such 'hoop' is regular attendance at church services. A prominent researcher on the nature of religious or spiritual experience for more than 25 years, Dr David Hay,

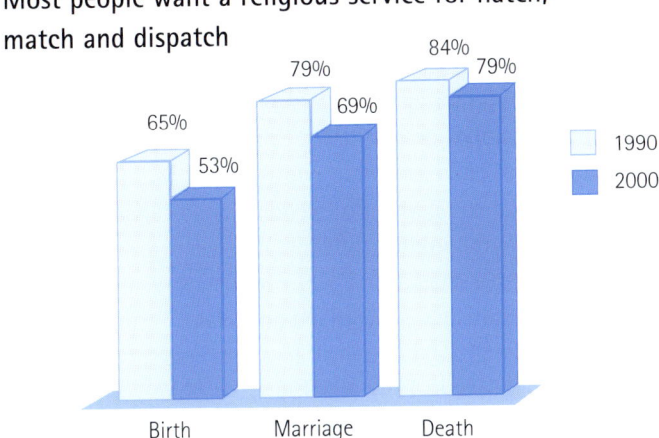

7. Most people want a religious service for hatch, match and dispatch

	Birth	Marriage	Death
1990	65%	79%	84%
2000	53%	69%	79%

Q. Do you personally think it is important to hold a religious service for any of the following events? *(ORB 2000)*

comments: 'Religion used to refer to the whole of the human encounter with the divine, but has shrivelled down to connote something like "churchgoing".'[33] Alongside this research view comes the voice of an experienced parish priest. Commenting on the growing evidence of cultural Christianity in our country, Canon Alan Billings observes that 'participation in church life is not seen as crucial for the practice of Christianity, and it is the practice of Christianity that British people think important. This is what makes a person a Christian, not churchgoing.'[34] In this context it is worth noting a recent study by the Catholic Church in England and Wales[35] which reported: 'It seems that church involvement is either becoming one choice among many or simply less of a viable option.' It continued to note that where church services times have changed and the number of services offered reduced it is 'more difficult for some families to continue to attend regularly. Families who do go to [church] regularly are making tremendous sacrifices to do so.' So churches must take care not to impose unrealistic expectations on those who come for the various rites of passage.

Social conformity is a strong pressure on most people in Britain today but the Church is perhaps guilty of adding its own pressure that has equally deterred interest, particularly among younger people. In 2004 the number of Church of England baptisms continued to decrease to 143,600, although, alongside traditional infant baptisms, this concealed a growing number of child and adult baptisms (for those over one year old). In the same year the number of weddings and services of blessing rose to 62,200, while the number of funerals exceeded the total of all these other 'rites of passage' at 212,500.[36] Statistics recorded by the Office for National Statistics for England and Wales[37] confirm that the proportion of weddings conducted within a religious service has been steadily falling from 51% in 1981 and 1991 to 32% in 2003. We have seen that there remains a God-shaped need in most people in Britain today to mark rites of passage through life with a religious service but the Church is not meeting that need.

Secularization

As we have looked at the religious and spiritual heart of Britain, we have seen that the trends of secularization have not overtaken our nation. This remains true in other parts of Europe too. Professor Grace Davie, writing in *Europe: The Exceptional Case*,[38] quotes the example of the Nordic countries where residual membership of the churches remains high 'despite the fact that attendance and assent to credal statements are some of the lowest in Europe'. 'Europeans', Davie says, 'seek and search within a framework of their historic churches, more often than not returning "home" when they die (Princess Diana being the most celebrated example).' Modern Danish society is an example of an established form of Christianity, where 85% of the population are tax-paying members of the church. Most of the population is baptized, confirmed and married at church and buried with the assistance of a clergy (wo)man. Yet Denmark is regarded as one of the most secularized societies where there is little understanding of the Christian story. In her study of faith in Europe, Davie summarizes such West Europeans as remaining 'by and large, unchurched populations rather

Listening to the nation

than simply secular.'[39] In separate pieces of research carried out for Tearfund and the Church of England in 2005,[40] a staggering three in ten of the adult population were found to have no experience of church (or Sunday School). This proportion rose to over half among young adults under 25 years of age. Around three in ten adults in modern-day Britain then are 'unchurched', in Davie's terms, and for these we must assume little inherent religious language or experience.

'Listening to the Nation' research has shown us that this does not imply a lack of spiritual or religious awareness. In the Nordic countries secularization is perhaps more advanced than in Britain, but Peter Skov-Jacobsen, writing of his experience as a pastor in Copenhagen,[41] feels

> there is a general openness towards the notion of religion and spirituality [but] not necessarily an acceptance of the Christian faith . . . It seems that ordinary secularized Danes must have a good excuse to go to church, and baptism is one of them.

Maybe this provides a pointer to the low level of religious literacy and the churchgoing malaise in Britain today? The companion booklet to this, entitled 'Churchgoing Today', also reveals that people will attend church on particular occasions. They need a reason to attend church and churches need to make such opportunities better known across their local communities.

Religion in the world today is often judged as becoming more secularized but the world is being de-secularized and faith is playing an increasing, though often misunderstood, public role. The key role of faith-based groups in the 2004 re-election of President Bush in the USA took many international observers by surprise. Since the turn of the millennium the political power of faith groups in other parts of the world has also grown at tremendous rates. Religious identity closer to home in Britain is also becoming more, not less, important as the British population

THE CHRISTIAN HEART OF BRITAIN REMAINS, IN SPITE OF SELECTIVE EVIDENCE IN RECENT YEARS TO THE CONTRARY, AND THE CHALLENGE TO THE CHURCHES IS TO MAKE THIS A MORE ACTIVE REALITY FOR THE TWENTY-FIRST CENTURY.

Christian roots, contemporary spirituality

diversifies in terms of religion and race. The religious and racial mix is becoming more complex, bringing a healthy vibrancy into a worn and tired religiosity.

A word of warning comes from a report by the Yorkshire and Humber Assembly in 2002 entitled 'Religious Literacy'. It comments that 'religious literacy is at a very low level – leading at times to religious discrimination, and sometimes to abuse and violence'. It found that agencies tend to relate to communities according to race and ethnicity rather than faith. One has only to look at the national daily newspapers to see evidence of these misunderstandings but multi-faith awareness is slowly increasing. The public and private Christian roots of our country are being re-evaluated by many at the beginning of the twenty-first century. Schools, for example, are noticing that many parents are beginning to value their Christian culture and inheritance again. The Christian heart of Britain remains, in spite of selective evidence in recent years to the contrary, and the challenge to the churches is to make this a more active reality for the twenty-first century.

> THE RELIGIOUS AND RACIAL MIX IS BECOMING MORE COMPLEX, BRINGING A HEALTHY VIBRANCY INTO A WORN AND TIRED RELIGIOSITY.

2

Listening to the local

In the previous chapter we listened to the voice of our nation as it reflected on its Christian roots. Now we shall turn to our local communities to see if we hear any different messages there. Do we hear any evidence of Christian roots in the everyday lives of those who live there? This chapter focuses on several key opportunities for religious participation in ordinary, everyday lives, namely churchgoing, Christmas, remembering and family occasions. We shall listen to what such occasions mean for individual lives in modern-day Britain and whether Christian roots of the local church can be there with any credibility.

Back to church

On 26 September 2004, the Anglican diocese of Manchester piloted 'Back to Church Sunday' across 160 churches. Churchgoers were equipped to invite a friend with credit-card-style invitations, posters, service resources and a welcome bag containing, among other things, a bar of donated Co-op Fair Trade chocolate. The idea proved to be a simple and effective way of reconnecting people with church. The diocesan evangelist said:

> This has been a very do-able way of developing a culture of invitation in our churches. There are loads of people who for whatever reason have lost touch with church, and who might be just waiting for an invitation to come again.

The Christian story of Christmas still attracts many people to church. Only young adults in their late teens and early twenties appear to be missing from Christmas congregations. At the turn of the millennium, over three in ten (33%) Britons attended church at Christmas.[6] When the survey was repeated in 2003, nearly four in ten (39%) attended church over the Christmas period and just two years later in 2005, the number had increased further to over four in ten (43%). There were slightly fewer men and young adults, but they came from all social classes and all areas of the country. They were more likely to be Roman Catholic or Free Church and they were more likely to live in rural areas, separate towns, suburban and inner-city areas. Back in 1990, the Rural Church Project[7] found approximately half (51%) of rural populations attended church at Christmas. City centre churches and those on council estates and in seaside areas have lower Christmas attendances but, even here, one in three adults attend church at Christmas. In London nearly half the population (48%) attend church at Christmas and the festival even attracts 22% of those from other faiths to their local church.

People attend church at Christmas for many different and diverse reasons. It may be nostalgia, the music, the candle-lit atmosphere, the children, personal comfort or seeking something more than the overpowering mid-winter festival of consumerism and partying. But they come! Any modern commercial enterprise would be jealous of such a large and loyal following. David Self, writing in the *Church Times*,[8] reminded readers of the comparable following for the over forty-year-old programme, the BBC *Songs of Praise*, which regularly gains an audience approaching five million. He cited an opinion poll conducted for the BBC back in 1954 when the People's Service on the Light Programme (today's Radio 2) regularly won four million listeners. People found the broadcasts 'comforting', 'helpful in coping with daily life', they 'reminded me of my younger days', in short, simple religion. This populist touch meets the needs of many and this, Self argues, should be our approach to Christmas in our churches.

Christmas roots

On Christmas Day and Christmas Eve 2004, Church of England parishes reported 2.6 million people in church, a figure slightly lower than the 2.9 million attending in the year of the new millennium. If this is repeated across all Christian denominations, approaching one in five people attend church over the Christmas 24 hours. In the Colchester area, the Anglican bishop made similar local enquiries at Christmas 2004. He discovered 11% of the rural population and 6% of the urban population in the area was at a Church of England church over the Christmas 24 hours. Again, overall, approaching one in five of the local population attended church on Christmas Day and Christmas Eve. Of the disparity between rural and urban Christmas attendance, Bishop Christopher Morgan observed that 'in rural areas the church continues to provide something of a community focus which is somewhat diluted in urban areas'.[9]

2004 average church attendance

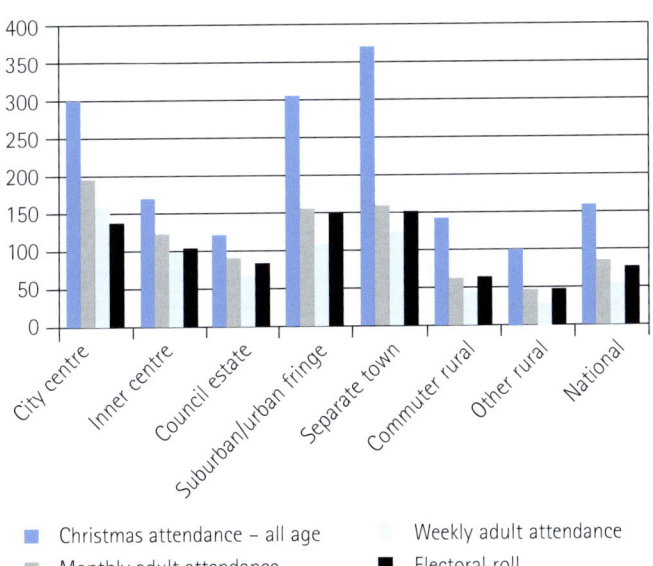

Christian roots, contemporary spirituality

Church of England national statistics show that church attendance on Christmas Day and Christmas Eve is between two and three times the levels of regular weekly church attendance. In 2003 local churches attracted congregations of, on average, 164 over the Christmas 24 hours compared to the average number of weekly attenders being 59 and the average Electoral Roll membership being 76. Even the estimate of people attending over a month (taken from the highest weekly number of attenders over a typical month) is only half the number attending on Christmas Day and Christmas Eve. The graph above shows how these figures vary in different parts of the country. Churches in towns, city centres and suburban areas see the largest Christmas congregations. Rural areas see the smallest but these are three times the weekly congregation in areas with populations of under 3,000. For churches in the inner city and on council estates, Christmas holds the least interest, perhaps just doubling the weekly congregation.

Cathedrals attract huge numbers to their Christmas services, often having to turn away people because of building health and safety considerations. Hereford Cathedral attracts 1,000 to its main carol service, 800 to a service for children and families on Christmas Eve and similar numbers at 'Carols for Shoppers', several school and fire brigade carol services. Rochester Cathedral broadcasts its main carol service into the cathedral close because of the high numbers wanting to attend. Other cathedrals now repeat the main carol service twice on consecutive days and these congregations are far from small. Chichester Cathedral now has two free but ticket-only evening carol services together with an open-door afternoon carol service. At Exeter Cathedral, for example, the main 'Grandisson' carol service attracts around 2,500 people and those queuing outside are frequently turned away because of the 'full house'. In London, Southwark Cathedral has seen its Christmas Day/Eve attendance increase by 45% over five years, from 1,181 in 2000 to 1,712 in 2005. In particular, attendance at its traditional crib service has increased from 65 to 616 in ten years from 1995 to 2005. However you look at Christmas attendances across the Church, there are many people of all ages who, year by year, return to their church roots at Christmas. For some it is intermingled with nostalgia and renewing ties with family and friends, while for others it may be part of a wider spiritual journey.

But Christmas also brings many tensions to the surface in our religiously pluralistic country. In December 2004, the *Sun* organized a campaign to 'Save Our Christmas', to see off the perceived threat of 'politically correct meanies'. It campaigned to keep the Christ in Christmas and, particularly, to keep nativity plays in schools. Several other newspapers joined the debate. The *Times Educational Supplement* discovered that 83% of primary schools hold nativity plays and 74% of schools hold carol services.[10] The *Times* headline was: 'We are committing cultural suicide', and continued, 'Christianity is being insidiously erased from the map.'[11] It cited the lack of a Christ-centred message on postage stamps and the decision to ban Christmas at the Eden Centre in Cornwall, preferring to call it 'A time with gifts'. Two or three years previously, the Church of England General Synod wrote to the Royal Mail suggesting some reflection of the Christian Christmas story on postage stamps. This request was met with a rebuff, making such a public defence of a Christian festival by national newspapers perhaps unique in modern times.

The Christmas debate became rather tangled as religious and national roots grew increasingly intertwined. 'We're all British. And Christmas is a British tradition', said Michael Howard, then leader of the Conservative Party.[12] The following year the debate rumbled on but Lambeth Council in London had to retreat on a decision to erect what it announced as winter lights for the Christmas period. The controversy was eased when it invited its leading Christian resident, the Archbishop of Canterbury, to switch on the by then renamed Christmas lights. The chairman of the Council for Racial Equality has gone on record to assure Christians that Christmas is 'not offensive to minority communities . . . nor is it racially exclusive . . . Most people of other faiths are bemused that we should even question it.'[13] Indeed, several non-Christian faith leaders have publicly endorsed this position. The Christmas season presents the most widespread opportunity for Christian witness in our country today. The residual, inherited faith in the Christian festival of Christmas, so evident in recent years, should challenge us to help people understand more of their Christian roots at Christmas.

Remembering

It is not only the annual Christmas festival that attracts people to church. There are other occasions that strike a chord with contemporary spirituality. Local churches know that when they put on a service for a special occasion, new people come to church. Whether it is a particular local occasion or a national event to mark, for example, the Queen's Golden Jubilee or the new millennium, local people are keen to attend church as part of the celebrations and to reflect on the meaning of the event for themselves and their community. At more sombre times too, people turn to the local church. Services to remember a local tragedy or to respond to a national disaster are also well attended. About 500 people attended a Road Peace Service at Hereford Cathedral for victims of road traffic accidents, their families and the emergency services, and a similar number attended a Tree of Light service for the bereaved in association with the local hospice. Church services on Remembrance Sunday have experienced a resurgence in recent years, attracting not only people affected by the two World Wars, but also those who have suffered from the increasing number of conflicts across our world in modern times. One in four people (27%) now attend church on Remembrance Sunday,[14] an increase from one in five (21%) in 2001 and it is the only regular Church 'festival' that attracts as many men as women, although most are aged 40 years or over.

Remembering is a key phenomenon in Britain today. Men and women spontaneously respond to tragedy by creating a place of remembrance with shared memories, pictures, flowers and candles. Such informal acts of mourning now frequently follow any innocent loss of life. It is not unusual to see flowers by a roadside or the scene of a crime turned into an informal shrine. After moments of national disaster we have

Listening to the local

come to expect an occasion of national remembrance. Soon after the London bombing in 2005, for example, additional services of remembrance were arranged near the sites of the atrocities for victims, families and friends. In recent years we have become a nation for whom memories and the remembrance of them, particularly with the loss of loved ones, is very important. In the last year nearly half (47%) of adults have attended a memorial service for someone who has died.[15] Only a few years ago, at the turn of the millennium, the number was under half of this (at 22%). Even more striking is the 56%, nearly three in five, who have attended a funeral in church (or maybe a Christian service in a local crematorium chapel).

> ONE IN FOUR PEOPLE (27%) NOW ATTEND CHURCH ON REMEMBRANCE SUNDAY, AN INCREASE FROM ONE IN FIVE (21%) IN 2001.

Occasions of Christian remembrance serve as important reminders of the God-given value of individual lives. When Torbay Council in Devon tried to remove the wooden cross from its chapel, funeral directors were infuriated and the story made the national newspapers. One funeral director said: 'Out of the last seventy funerals I have organized at the crematorium only three or four have been non-religious services. Most people expect to see a cross in place.' Another added: 'It is a chapel. It was dedicated as a Christian chapel by the bishop at the time.'[16] The opportunity to mark a departure from this life with a Christian funeral remains very important and many clergy are beginning to grasp its significance in the spiritual and religious searching among those who mourn. Professor Grace Davie has observed that the established Church, in particular, is expected to be there for just such occasions, whether the deceased has led an unequivocal Christian life or not.[17]

The purpose of memorializing is not to glorify the dead but rather to speak to the living. By remembering, recollecting and recalling, we are doing more than merely reminding. We pledge ourselves to each other and to God, where we receive hope for the future and are equipped to face the task of living anew. There is a fine line to be trodden between remembering a good life and elevating the deceased to sainthood, between allowing secular memories and sidelining any Christian message. The use of popular modern music is often contentious but it is salutary to note that one of the most popular songs played at funerals in recent years is entitled 'Angels' by Robbie Williams,[18] a particular mix of sentimentality, religious and spiritual imagery. Co-operative Funeralcare reported in November 2005 that 40% of all pieces of music chosen for funerals were popular songs, 5% were classical but the majority, 55%, were hymns. There is, however, no doubt that modern-day funerals, memorial services and other acts of remembrance generate many opportunities for local churches to engage with local communities. Clergy who have little help from their parishes can find the funeral load hard work, for we know that parish clergy conduct, on average, two funerals every month and that half of all deaths involve such support by the local parish and clergy. For those who remember, memorial services and funerals can be key moments of spiritual and religious reflection in their lives. The challenge before us is that at such times most people continue to want the local church to draw alongside and offer support.

> THE CHALLENGE BEFORE US IS THAT AT SUCH TIMES MOST PEOPLE CONTINUE TO WANT THE LOCAL CHURCH TO DRAW ALONGSIDE AND OFFER SUPPORT.

Family occasions

So, by listening to our local communities we find that our final rite of passage presents the most frequent point of contact that families and friends have with the local church. With modern family life becoming increasingly fragmented, it is not entirely obvious whether there are many other opportunities for local churches to engage with different models of family life. Listening to what is going on around us in British society becomes even more important and perhaps surprisingly we find that family is still very important to us. Four in five (80%) would say that their family was their main source of identity.[19] It is more important than any other aspect of our lives, including social background (31%), nationality (27%), place of birth (27%), language (22%), religious background (15%), ethnic background (14%), school/university (20%) and even football team

(6%). And yet, the traditional family is increasingly becoming out of fashion. The 2001 government census found 59% of parents in households with children are married, 11% are co-habiting and 22% are lone-parent families. In 2003 over 40% of children were born outside marriage, a figure that has increased steadily from 10% in the 1970s. More than half of couples divorcing had at least one child under the age of sixteen while a quarter of all births were to couples who lived together but were not married.[20]

Families are also becoming smaller and are started much later in life. Marriages last on average for eleven-and-a-half years and four in ten end in divorce, with the highest divorce rate being among men and women in their twenties. By 2031, government actuaries predict that nearly half of men and more than a third of women in their mid-forties will not have walked up the aisle.[21] It will not be divorce that seriously impacts many children in the future but parents moving in and out of different relationships in which marriage is not a factor. In spite of all this, a recent survey among 18- to 21-year-olds found that 77% still felt that marriage was a 'realistic lifetime commitment'.[22] Over 70% expected to get married and over half (54%) felt that living together did not offer the same commitment. Phillip Hodson, a fellow of the British Association for Counselling and Psychotherapy, suggested that when a couple marry they become more interdependent. 'Marriage is when two people become one', he suggested, 'and cohabitation is when two people remain two.'[23] Without any direct reference to the Christian lifestyle, in this survey men and women reveal equal confidence that 'it is possible to be in love with one person for life' and agree that 'most people do not work hard enough on their marriages'. Seven in ten men and seven in ten women agreed with each of these statements and also with the aim that 'finding someone to love and who loves us is the most important thing in life'.[24] With the average cost of a wedding currently put at about £17,250[25] (and even at £300 per head for the wedding guests[26]), it is clear that couples want to mark this key rite of passage in their lives with a significant occasion, but perhaps it will not be long before these prospective brides and bridegrooms may find it all too expensive.

> FOR MANY UNMARRIED COUPLES, THE BAPTISM HAS TAKEN THE PLACE OF THE WEDDING AS THE FIRST PUBLIC EVENT THAT THEY CELEBRATE AS A COUPLE.

Marriage is certainly less common today and divorce more prevalent. In 1991, approximately 300,000 marriages were conducted in England, half of which were Christian ceremonies. Just ten years later in 2002, there were about 250,000 marriages but only a third were religious ceremonies. The picture improves among first marriages (representing about 60% of all marriages) in that the proportion of religious ceremonies only decreased across these ten years from two-thirds to just under a half. God seems to be excluded from most modern marriages, but there was indignation in the national press when readings mentioning God and even songs with spiritual elements, such as Robbie Williams's 'Angels', were banned from civil weddings. Bishops subsequently caught the mood of the nation in calling on the General Register Office 'for a somewhat more generous approach'[27], and in due course the ban was lifted. Baptisms, like marriages, are on the decline but Canon Alan Billings, writing in the *Church Times*,[28] observed that baptism parties are getting bigger because for many unmarried couples, 'the baptism has taken the place of the wedding as the first public event that they celebrate as a couple ... It is a rite of passage for them as much as for the child.' All this affects the churches' response to baptisms and marriages, not least because the local congregation can be taken over by regular baptism services and local church buildings can only seat so many people. If baptism parties are growing in size, the number of baptisms at any one church service has to be limited!

In 2001 an ecumenical survey was conducted in England across local Protestant churches. When the Church of England results were analysed, it was found that 5% of churchgoers had joined their local church after attending a wedding, baptism or funeral service.[29] These services remain a helpful link with those who have drifted away from church and can be instrumental in rekindling their faith. Congregations and ministers must work together to maximize these links with members of their local community who are tentatively exploring the Christian foundations of family life.

So often, the church is perceived to deter such enquiries because of the widening communication gap between ordinary families and their local parish clergy. Ordinary church members can be particularly effective in responding to cautious approaches to include God in their family occasion, as many churches with properly trained baptism and marriage preparation teams and bereavement support have discovered. Local churches must respond to the spiritual needs of those they serve with increasing imagination. Thanksgiving services for the birth of a child, blessings of marriage, the renewal of wedding vows, services of reconciliation and remembering may be more appropriate in certain circumstances. These stepping stones towards a deeper faith involve faith conversations that must be nurtured carefully by churches working closely with the local community. The traditional rites of passage can still present a modern-day window to kindle the flame of Christian faith in the heart of family life.

So, the role of churches in Christian services of baptism, marriage and funerals is increasingly to encourage Christian faith and practice in family life. After a service of baptism, one mother said to Canon Billings in front of her partner: 'This is the first time I have got him to talk about the future of our family. Thank you.' All this puts far from traditional interpretations on church attendance for rites of passage but it explains a great deal about contemporary expectations of local churches.

In surveys conducted for the Church of England between 2001 and 2005,[30] large increases were found among those who attended baptisms, weddings and funerals. The number of adults attending funerals in the previous year remained at around 56% while the number attending baptisms in the previous year rose from 29% to 41% (over four in ten) and the number of adults attending weddings in the previous year rose from 39% to 51%, over a half. Both baptisms and weddings are less common but their social impact is increasing as each rite of passage diversifies in its social significance. What is more, these two Christian

> THE TRADITIONAL RITES OF PASSAGE CAN STILL PRESENT A MODERN-DAY WINDOW TO KINDLE THE FLAME OF CHRISTIAN FAITH IN THE HEART OF FAMILY LIFE.

ceremonies attract as many men as women and more young adults than older ones, which is surely a rarity in church life. They are popular across the country in rural and urban areas, in towns and, surprisingly, they are most popular of all in city centres.

We are accustomed to celebrating family life on occasions such as Mothering Sunday and about one in six (16%) of the population continue to attend church on this family 'festival', a proportion that has remained fairly static in recent years. But local experience and the statistics tell us that we need to look wider at the growing opportunities to bring the relevance of the Christian faith into family life on occasions of birth, marriage and death. Family occasions are important rites of passage for all concerned. 'Priests and congregations should rejoice that so many people understand themselves to be Christian and seek their sacred places for the various rites of passage.'[31] 'Listening to the Local' has revealed the Christian heartbeat still within contemporary family and community life. Many people are surprisingly open to their local churches for particular occasions. Christmas, of course, brings all this together as local churches find themselves for a period of the year the focal point of local community life, where people remember and reflect on the holy family. How each church can best use this seasonal window of opportunity depends on the local community, its history and its stories that only you can research!

3

Listening to the past

Public faith

Many people feel that the Church is living in the past and that it wants to have control, whereas today, people 'don't so much want to be told what to believe as to be shown how.'[1] 'Despite a general goodwill towards Christians and Christian faith, the popular perception of Church may therefore be that it is in conflict with spiritual growth and development.'[2] Such statements as these are a wake-up call to the churches. In recent discussions concerning public faith, Martyn Percy has considered the journey of British Charismatic Christianity. This attracts a considerable following, from being a movement to a church with order and rituals,[3] in contrast to the religious landscape in the West, which is seen to be shifting from the institution to the individual.

The church historian, Adrian Hastings, remarked at the close of the twentieth century: 'Our age . . . is one of the secularization of society and the desecularization of religion . . . Only when religion has adjusted to [this] can it effectively resume its missionary task.'[4] Since then, religious plurality has grown apace but the authority of the Church remains today as secondary to personal experiences, the Bible and human reason.[5] Indeed, for some, the church 'is a barrier rather than an aid to their relationship with God'. Authority is shifting from 'without' to 'within'. The self, rather than traditions, has become the ultimate reference point in the lives of individuals. Traditions still exist, but they are losing their scope and influence.

How has this situation come about? It is worth looking back, listening to the past in order to reflect on the present. Public faith in Britain has been in decline for most of the twentieth century. The high point in terms of church attendance for the Church of England was in 1851. It has been estimated that 40% of the population were in church for Mothering Sunday that year, when the only comprehensive church attendance census was carried out across England and Wales.[6] For urban Anglicans, church attendance decline began very soon after this, for Free Churches it began soon after 1870 and among Roman Catholics soon after 1960. At the beginning of the twentieth century, approximately 60% of the population were nominally (baptized and married) Church of England[7] while between 25% and 40% were in church each Sunday, of whom half were Anglican.

Church of England allegiance was stronger in the rural south and Free Church membership stronger in the industrial north. Approximately 15% were Free Church, 5% Roman Catholic and 5% of no religion. Churchgoing was weakest in the north (especially in the established church) where, after the Industrial Revolution, the majority of working-class town populations in the north did not go to church. The Church of England, in particular, was at the beginning of the twentieth century already developing 'a considerably smaller total constituency, but of a higher sacramental commitment within the constituency'.[8] Then, across the twentieth century, all the official longitudinal and long-running statistics of the Church of England for baptisms, confirmations, marriages, stipendiary clergy, electoral rolls, Easter and Christmas communicants, usual Sunday attendance, adult and child, show overall significant decline. Free Church membership figures also declined, being highly dependent on the vigour of Sunday Schools, which suffered dramatically following the 1902 Education Act and the improvement of weekday schools.

This decline has accelerated since the 1960s when, Callum Brown[9] argues, organized Christianity was sent 'on a downward spiral to the margins of social significance' by the 'swinging sixties'. His thesis is that large-scale disaffection with organized religion is primarily a post-war phenomenon due to broad cultural changes over which the churches have no direct control. Christianity over a thousand years became embedded in the ordinary lives of people in Britain. With each generation it was renewed and it adapted to social and cultural contexts that arose. It survived the Reformation, the Enlightenment and the Industrial Revolution but, Brown argues, the very core of the nation's religious culture has been irrevocably eroded by the rise in secularization.

The statistics of church membership over the 1960s certainly make gloomy reading. Free Church membership dramatically fell by over 20% (Baptist churches being the exception at 13%), Church of England confirmations fell by over 40%, Church of England baptisms (per thousand live births) fell by 16% and Roman Catholic decline began.[10] Some comfort to Brown's prophecy of doom is offered by Professor Alister McGrath, who observes that atheism has not run its course and, at the beginning of the twenty-first century, 'secularization, far from replacing religion, is itself in decline'.[11]

In recent years there has been the progressive disengagement of religious institutions from public life and the increasing differentiation of the religious and secular spheres. The status of religion in Britain is progressively reverting to a private religion of individual experience. Religion has always been a deeply personal experience but it is now increasingly private. It generally lacks social significance and certainly is no longer a means of social control. In 2001 the number of baptized Anglicans fell below half that of the population of England.[12] Among people in England over 50 years of age, more than 60% were baptized Church of England as infants; by the 1970s this had dropped to under half and by 2000 the proportion was only one in five. In recent years there has been an increasing trend for people to be baptized later in life and a growing number participate in the alternative (and preparatory) service of thanksgiving for a child so that 'it is not altogether absurd to wonder in what senses that statistics of baptism are measuring the same phenomenon over time'.[13] However, this diversification is not enough significantly to alter the overall impact of baptized Church of England members. If current trends continue, it will not be many years before baptized Christians are in a minority.

Christian roots, contemporary spirituality

IN OUR CONVERSATIONS WITH MODERN-DAY BRITONS WE CAN NO LONGER TAKE THE CHRISTIAN STORY FOR GRANTED.

The demise of public faith is of concern because public faith informs private faith. Britain is moving away from institutions and formal religion. It is losing the inherited language and symbols of Christianity. Approximately three in ten of the population are estimated to be 'unchurched'[14] in that they have never attended church or Sunday School regularly. This is alongside five in ten, half, who are 'de-churched' in that they no longer attend church regularly. In our conversations with modern-day Britons we can no longer take the Christian story for granted. Many today would say 'I am not religious . . . [but] I definitely believe in something.' 'The danger is that without a shared language, spirituality will continue to be privatized. Individuals . . . will not know how to share that with others.'[15] With the loss of public faith comes the need to recover a public spirituality. 'Religion without spirituality is dead. Spirituality without religion tends to drift loose from its moorings . . . It is too easily led astray.'[16]

Believing without belonging

Britain aligns itself with Europe. The EEC constitution may be under review, but we share much of our history with Europe. Part of this history is the constitutional connections between Church and State. Europeans seek and search within the framework of their historic churches, a backdrop that is unique across the world. Anglicanism thrives globally and other world religions are growing in Britain, so does the history of Christianity in Europe encumber modern-day faith? Canon Professor Grace Davie has made some useful reflections on the evolving Christian scene across Europe that will aid our reflection.

There are many ways of measuring the religiosity of a population and, in the widely recognized European Values Study, denominational allegiance, church attendance, attitudes towards the Church, indicators of religious belief and religious disposition are all examined. This, along with socio-economic data, presents a rich and complex matrix of religious life. No single variable can be taken to judge the strength or health of religious practice. Sadly, today, we easily fall into this trap, often taking church attendance, in particular, as the barometer of church life. We must examine variables that are concerned with feelings, experience and the more numinous religious beliefs as well as those that measure religious orthodoxy, ritual participation and institutional attachment. Secularization has brought to western Europe a decline in the latter whereas the former persists. Grace Davie describes religious life in Europe as one of 'believing without belonging',[17] a term that has attracted much attention and discussion. She challenges the unqualified reference to secularization, preferring 'to suggest that Western Europeans remain, by and large, unchurched populations rather then simply secular'.[18]

This view resonates with many who have pastoral contact beyond the gathered church and among those who observe national religious life. Others would want to add that the residual Christian faith evident today is an 'inherited folk religion' involving little commitment. We are all aware of the rise in Islam and of the vitality of religion in many parts of Africa and in the Indian subcontinent. In modern times Europe has become a place with different faiths competing for public space. This in itself may encourage innovation and bring religious vitality in new ways in the coming years.

> IN MODERN TIMES EUROPE HAS BECOME A PLACE WITH DIFFERENT FAITHS COMPETING FOR PUBLIC SPACE.

Religious capital

In Britain today there is increasing interest among government policy makers in the religious and social capital that faith communities bring to their local areas in terms of its religious life. The saying, 'Say one for me, vicar', is hardly new and its use still persists in some (mainly rural) areas. Farming families, for example, frequently rely almost entirely on the matriarch of the family to represent them in local church life. This arises from practical necessity when every daylight hour must be spent on the land, weather permitting. But it also indicates the persistence of vicarious religion where people rely on a minority of churches and churchgoers to enact a memory on their behalf. 'People then draw on this religious capital at crucial times in their individual or their collective lives.'[19] Certainly, there are many farming families who fiercely support the local church and would expect the vicar to call at significant times in their lives but who only attend church services at Harvest and Christmas and in that order of importance. The high take-up of religious ceremonies at the time of death is also indicative of this phenomenon on a broader scale.

At the beginning of the twenty-first century we have seen an emerging role for our churches, cathedrals and church leaders at times of national and local crisis. The parish churches in Boscastle, Cornwall and Soham, Cambridgeshire took centre stage in the immediate aftermath of the recent tragedies in their towns. In July 2005 people immediately turned to the parish church in Tavistock Square, London following the bus bombing there. Davie again articulates this concept as follows, pointing out the rarity of vicarious religion outside Europe: 'Europeans, by and large, regard their churches as public utilities rather than competing firms; this is the real legacy of state church history and inextricably related to the concept of vicariousness.'[20]

We can take the notions of vicarious religion and 'believing without belonging' a stage further with reference to our consumer society. As the social norms attached to religious life are disappearing and nominal attachment lessens, there is increased polarization between churchgoers and non-churchgoers. Returning to Davie again, we are encouraged by her to see this as a result of the move from obligation to consumption as instanced by the dramatic decrease in teenage confirmation and infant baptism numbers at the same time as adult confirmations and baptisms are rising. 'Voluntarism (a market) is beginning to establish itself, de facto, regardless of the constitutional position of the churches.'[21] This may mean that vicariousness ceases to be the norm but, Davie continues, 'emergent voluntarism is as conditioned by the past (including the presence of a state church) as its precedents'. Again the confirmation service provides a good example. This teenage rite of passage is now a relatively rare event undertaken, as a matter of personal choice, at any age to make a public declaration of faith. 'It is an opportunity to make public what has often been an entirely private activity ... confirmation becomes an "experience" in addition to a rite of passage implying a better fit with other aspects of youth culture.'[22]

Our inheritance

By listening to the past, we have traced the increased privatization of religion in Britain to a faith today of individual choice and practice. We have observed the decline in the role of public faith in Britain that has left a residual Christian culture that emerges more strongly at times of significance or crisis. As previous chapters have shown, the religious capital in local communities and in the nation is real, but we can now see that it is gradually diminishing as more and more Britons have little direct experience of the Christian faith or rely on an increasingly distant inherited faith. Churches must develop a faith vocabulary that has meaning to the significant numbers of 'unchurched' and 'dechurched' in our country today, those who have never attended church regularly and those who no longer do so.

Research has helped us to listen carefully to the messages of modern-day Britain to local churches and now we must respond. We need to bring the research directions together to guide the churches in which you and I are involved as they grapple with the shifting community around them. That is the purpose of the final chapter to which we now turn. We shall look at the common messages and further unwrap the surprises we find as we explore how the local church can respond to the research challenges we have uncovered.

4

Surprising signs of the times

Following the research into Britain's Christian roots has taken us in several directions. 'Listening to the Nation', 'the Local' and 'the Past' has affirmed the role of the local church in Britain today and has provided signposts for churches to follow in today's world. We are used to being told that the local church is in decline, but more considered reflection on the research evidence has shown us how premature this judgement is. Churches are valued by the people of Britain for the religious value they bring to our country and yet there is a gulf in the conversation between the British and their churches. To help us bridge this gap it is crucial that the research signposts are brought together to see the common directions they provide to your church and mine.

There have been some common threads emerging as you and I have listened to the research, and it is time to bring them together. Initially we shall consider how to respond to the first surprises from our listening exercise: the modern-day mission challenge posed by prayer and spirituality, memories and their symbols. Then we shall follow the research surprises showing the importance of Christmas and family specials in the lives of our neighbours. Further surprises emerge as local churches respond in different ways to these challenges in their local community. Listening to the research, to local stories and reflecting together will provide fresh signposts for every church to follow their own God-given paths into the future.

Surprising signs of the times

Prayer and authentic spirituality

The importance of personal prayer in individual lives is one of the best-kept secrets in modern Britain. We may not all be as prayerful as we would like but it is very important to us. Most people pray and many pray regularly every week. The first surprise from 'Listening to the Nation' research is that prayer is a spiritual experience that most people both have and want. Clergy frequently find that people are grateful for prayer but embarrassment and vulnerability deter the request. 'Listening to the Nation' research has shown us that, although many New Age experiences are tried alongside prayer, none come near as being important in the lives of individuals.

The Church needs to listen to the nation's need for prayer. One of the few self-generated movements in the UK in recent years is the '24/7 Prayer Movement'. Its web site[1] currently has over 32,000 prayer requests posted on its 'Wailing Wall'. Many churches know at first hand the moving contributions on their own prayer boards; for passers-by always contribute to prayer stations, prayer trees or take the opportunity to light a candle in prayer.

With the rise in spiritual awareness comes a greater appetite for prayer and for silence both in church worship and at the fringes of church life. Contributors to 'The Mystery Worshipper' web site maintained by the 'Ship of Fools', frequently refer to the atmosphere during worship. One said: 'A moment or two of silence so profound you could hear your hair growing.' Much of our church worship is in danger of being pure entertainment and at times even emotional self-fulfilment when what people are often seeking is quiet prayerful spirituality and a sense of mystery. Bishop John Finney refers to this problem when he says:

> The world outside the Church has already discerned this truth about the Church: it is not spiritual enough. The world looks for spirituality and the Church does not satisfy that

> MUCH OF OUR CHURCH WORSHIP IS IN DANGER OF BEING PURE ENTERTAINMENT AND AT TIMES EVEN EMOTIONAL SELF-FULFILMENT WHEN WHAT PEOPLE ARE OFTEN SEEKING IS QUIET PRAYERFUL SPIRITUALITY AND A SENSE OF MYSTERY.

need. As Archbishop Michael Ramsey said, 'We have been dosing our people with religion, when what they want is not that, but a relationship with the living Lord.'[2]

A national journalist in turn echoes these thoughts: 'The Church of England has become the church of social commentators, confining its opinions to secular topics such as poverty or unemployment because it is too embarrassed to talk about God.'[3] God, the Holy Spirit, speaks to all creation, not just people who we judge to have 'got it right' religiously, but the Church is tasked with pointing people to the source of their spiritual experiences. Isolated spiritual experiences may be assumed a private possession and self-centred spirituality can be dangerous. Our corporate church worship will offer authentic spirituality when it shows a right balance between mystery and accessibility.

There are many forms of Christian prayer that are gaining in popularity in churches focused on mission:

- St Thomas's, Lancaster organized a 'prayer marathon' when congregation members prayed night and day for two weeks in preparation for Christmas. More than a hundred people prayed for an hour at a time, encouraged by the vicar to be creative as they prayed. The room set aside had candles and banners added, the walls became covered in prayer and pictures and the young prayed 'with loud music bouncing off the walls.'[4]

- Other churches have visited local residents in particular areas offering to pray the following Sunday for their street and any particular needs. A prayer card is offered and the response warm. Pastoral sensitivity has been paramount but links with the church neighbourhood have significantly developed.

- For those who like active prayer, the growing popularity of 'prayer labyrinths' and 'prayer stations' may attract attention.[5] Prayer stations allow 'prayer beyond words' through doing rather than speaking and seeing rather than hearing. They can incorporate touch and smell, so helping us to respond to God through all our senses. This idea has been taken successfully into church services to make prayer accessible to everyone and encourage real participation. It has been used for specific events and 'prayer fayres' that can take local, topical, moral or spiritual themes. Mark Rylands, Canon Missioner at Exeter Cathedral, emphasizes the importance of mission being planted in prayer. Many have been enthused for prayer-based mission at the Exeter prayer schools where interactive forms of prayer and intercessions have been introduced using everyday and biblical imagery.

   Prayer station at Wakefield cathedral

- The idea of prayer stations can be developed further in the great outdoors to form 'prayer walks'. Churches that take seriously their prayer life for the whole parish, have found prayer walks around the parish to be very helpful. Directions and pointers to prayer are vital, but this too encourages prayer with our eyes and other senses. 'Walks of witness' at Easter when all the local churches join together and walk behind the cross (on Good Friday) or the donkey (on Palm Sunday) can be used in this way. In rural areas traditional services at rogation times involving 'beating the bounds' have this potential too.

Christian roots, contemporary spirituality

Prayer Labyrinth at Portsmouth Cathedral

- Prayer labyrinths proved popular at an outreach event organized by Churches Together in Exeter entitled 'Life on the Beach', after the nickname given to the open space at the cathedral west front. Four Saturdays were chosen in May and June 2004 and four different environmental themes were taken. The huge labyrinth dominated the cathedral forecourt and attracted much interest. Performers and creative displays engaged the onlookers while those who participated in the prayer tree and the prayer labyrinth showed themselves open to spiritual exploration. Offra House, retreat centre for the Diocese of Coventry, offers a labyrinth resource kit for local churches to borrow and use. The laminated footprints can be used indoors or outside and when the kit was first used it formed a prayer trail through Coventry Cathedral ruins. Those feeling more ambitious can also use the Proost (Youth for Christ) labyrinth to create a multi-media labyrinth experience.

Surprising signs of the times

- Prayer boards and prayer candles have traditionally been a means of offering special intercessory prayer for individuals. Requests are included in the church's daily prayer life and the candle smoke symbolizes the prayers being carried to God. It is noticeable how casual visitors frequently make use of these opportunities. Candles have become popular today to bring calm and peace into a home or to create an intimate atmosphere. These are qualities we can beneficially bring to prayer and to church services. A quiet Taizé-style service, Eucharist or meditation in, for example, Holy Week or Advent all benefit with the use of candles to focus minds and hearts in the quiet alongside music, readings and prayer.

Memories and their symbols

The second surprise is that 'Listening to the Nation' research has shown how important memorial services and formal rituals of memory are in modern-day Britain but along with formal memorial services are the growing number of informal shrines where personal symbols are used to make memories public. Symbolism and ritual are aspects of modern spirituality where churches can show that they were there first. Icons in worship, pictures in stained glass and different forms of religious ritual were vital to non-literate people. Strangely, we have almost journeyed full circle to be a society highly dependent on visual imagery. Radio and books have a hard

Roadside Shrine

Christian roots, contemporary spirituality

battle competing with television and computers and so 'we are re-discovering the value of the iconic and the symbolic'.[6]

Modern spirituality has adopted symbolism in a big way. Roadside shrines often include teddies, flowers and other symbolic mementos. When two teenage girls were recently attacked and one murdered, their schoolmates created a shrine of flowers, teddies and school ties on the park bench where the attack took place. This phenomenon is not confined to this country. Across the world, in Russia, a memorial service was held for the 130 hostages killed when terrorists laid siege to School Number 1, Beslan. Grieving relatives brought water and bread to symbolize the food and water of which their children were deprived during the siege. Nine months after the siege, the burnt-out shell of the school gym remained as a shrine, with bottles of water and bouquets placed against the walls and on the floor.[7]

> To communicate with people today, we need to take as much everyday imagery as possible into our church worship and our explorations in prayer.

To communicate with people today, we need to take as much everyday imagery as possible into our church worship and our explorations in prayer. Some of our church services have liturgies which, if allowed to speak for themselves, do just this. Holy communion and baptism are pivotal examples but there are many opportunities in the church year. The drama of the Easter, the Passover and Christmas stories can be acted out or the symbols involved placed in view as the story is retold. On such occasions a sermon or talk can be superfluous. St David's, Exeter took five Lenten evenings to contemplate and then take part in an act of creativity. These evenings attracted visitors who valued the 'space for holiness'. It was a moving moment as the offerings created were blessed and laid on the chancel steps or pinned to the cross.

The use of spiritual symbols to aid private prayer and meditation is also growing in popularity today. A small portable cross or picture is not only useful for the sick but anyone seeking God's healing. A bracelet made for the Lutheran Church of Sweden has

Surprising signs of the times

become a surprise bestseller. More than 100,000 'Pearls of Life' bracelets have been sold in the past ten years. Each of the twelve round and six oblong beads is designed to represent a life-question or idea or prayer. The designer, Bishop Lonnebo said: 'It struck me that evangelical Christianity doesn't have any praying aids to help us stay focused.'[8] The beads resemble a rosary or the type of prayer beads used in the Eastern Churches. A book accompanies them and from Scandinavian countries they have found their way to Germany, America and Britain.[9]

Pearls of Life beads

Christmas

The residual Christian faith in the British Christmas today is the third surprise from the 'Listening to the Local' research, and symbolism has also found its way into Christmas. In 1968 The Children's Society was inspired to borrow an old Moravian tradition and the mystery created by the service has become an essential ingredient in the celebrations before or after Christmas for numerous children and their families. In 2004, The Children's Society received donations from over one million people who had exchanged their money for a symbolically decorated orange. Five thousand Christingle services raised over £1.1 million for the work of The Children's Society.[10] At these Christingle services many more enjoy the experience of this magical service alongside them and even more receive the symbolic orange at services without making any monetary contribution. Christingle services have caught the popular imagination and rival only carol services in their popularity. Schools and churches may adapt the service for their own use but the spiritual message in Christingle, Christ the light of the world, is shared and accepted by millions. Christingle touches a spiritual chord with many

Christian roots, contemporary spirituality

non-churchgoers and highlights the needs of those children (and others) who are neglected throughout the year.

One Devon village church resisted the trend for a Christingle service for years as it was committed to providing a successful children's nativity service that attracted over a hundred adults and children. When finally a Christingle service was held for the first time, it attracted a congregation of 175 while attendance at the nativity only dropped to 80. Coincidentally a special open-air nativity was also staged that year and a staggering three hundred attended, leaving standing room only for many. A fresh approach to traditional nativity plays frequently catches the imagination of local communities. Open-air plays and live donkeys do not have to be reserved for Easter. The Christingle service at Brackley Parish Church in Peterborough diocese has become so popular, it is held three times: on Christmas Eve at 2 pm, 3.15 pm and 4.30 pm.[11] The regular Sunday congregation is 120 but the church is packed for such special occasions as this. Last year the church put on a special harvest festival incorporating the local school. It was entitled 'Harvestingle' and was so successful that the name has stuck.

The traditions of Christmas and Christingle attract widespread participation at every level of society. 'Listening to the Local' research has shown the tremendous opportunities there are at Christmas to strengthen the memory of Christmas in our communities. However, with each generation the gospel must be renewed and its conversation with society re-established. In December 2004 a carol service was broadcast across the north-west region of England. It featured Cliff Richard, Russell Watson and the Bishop of Manchester. Thousands of people watched the broadcast in pubs, residential homes, hospitals and prisons. Many of the 150 churches that took part reported running out of seating and having to use overflow rooms.[12]

Churches are beginning to turn the secularization of Christmas around towards the Christ in Christmas. Almost half the population (49%) buy a Christmas tree at Christmas. This is as many as make a charitable donation (49%) and almost as many as listen to the Queen's speech (51%).[13] So churches around the country including Hampshire, Sussex and Devon have seized on a variation of the much-loved concept of flower festivals, a 'Christmas Tree festival'. Trees are sponsored and decorated by community groups, schools and local shops. It's a year-long project backed with lots of publicity but it brings many new faces into church. Holy Trinity, Cuckfield found 1,500 people visited over three days and they made a profit that was donated to a local charity. There were information leaflets and an activity sheet for children. The church contributed four parish trees illustrating baptisms, weddings, funerals and prayer. One visitor commented: 'The prayer tree brought tears to my eyes.' All in all, 48 trees were squeezed in, with another twelve decorating the window sills.[14]

St Mary's, Arnold, near Nottingham, could be said to save its best idea until after Christmas. It holds a 'Ceremony of Light' in the season of Epiphany. The service concludes as the Light of Christ is symbolically carried into the darkened church. As readings and prayers are said, the Christ candle is lit, followed by apostle candles and congregation candles. During the final hymn everyone processes with their candles into the church hall. This service has become such a local tradition over the last 20 years or so that 150 people can confidently be expected to attend even in the post-Christmas lull, and the church is able to use this service to build on contacts made at Christmas and the Christingle service. The use of candles and lights can be used at any time of the year beyond the Christmas season to encourage reflection, prayer and positive spiritual awareness, as one church in the Manchester diocese discovered when it turned Hallowe'en for good by introducing a children's party called 'Lite-Nite'.

Christian roots, contemporary spirituality

Family specials

Christmas is full of surprises. It is a special time for adults and children although it can be a difficult time for some. Of the population, 4%, mostly the elderly and the bereaved, will spend Christmas alone.[15] Many churches make special efforts to support these people and the good work undertaken by church members at a funeral can also be built on at such times; but the loss of a loved one can be particularly sharp at other times of the year too.

'Listening to the Nation' research has shown how important memorial services are to the bereaved and many clergy know this at first hand. One of the research surprises is the growing opportunities for the Christian faith in times of bereavement. Bereavement services provide an opportunity for loved ones to be remembered and can be a helpful part of learning to live with a bereavement. The herb, rosemary, has traditionally been associated with remembering and some churches have named their annual bereavement service, 'The Rosemary Service', while others focus on particular charities: for example, The Marie Curie service. Traditionally, such services are conducted around All Saints/All Souls tide. Invitations are sent to the recently bereaved and, during the service, congregation members light candles or, perhaps, flowers are planted in memory of those whom we see no more. Such short, simple services can provide helpful support after the funeral, particularly for those left with spiritual questions. The New Romney churches hold an annual service of memories that attracts over 300 people, including 50 aged under sixteen. The local undertakers would like the churches to hold the service more frequently and the local churches find it one of the most successful parts of their outreach ministry. Many who attend say they have nowhere to go to remember but they discover they are not alone in their grieving and much mutual support grows.

'Listening to the Local' research also shows a fourth surprise in the continuing but changing key role of rites of passage in the lives of many. The use of appropriate symbols in baptisms, marriages and funerals can be very helpful and results in very moving moments.

Surprising signs of the times

At the funeral of a young girl killed tragically in a road accident, her brothers and sisters placed mementoes of special memories onto her coffin as particular prayers were read. At St Mary's, Mirfield, the Paschal Candle by the coffin is lit as a prayer reminding the congregation of the resurrection hope in Christ is read. At the end of the service the members of the congregation are invited in turn to light a candle from the Paschal Candle and place it on the altar,[16] making a powerful symbolic Christian statement.

From the 'Listening to the Local' research, we know how important family life is to the majority. The surprise attraction of family specials can be broadened across the church year when there are many opportunities to use the commercial family 'festivals' (and their associated symbolism) inherent in Britain today. Bishop James Jones has suggested a twelve-month liturgical cycle to connect commercial opportunities with spiritual ones.[17] Several of these yearly 'festivals' focus on family relationships, with reminders of the Christian message at their origins.

January – New Year Resolutions – Repentance and New Promises

February – Valentine's Day – Celebration of Love

March – Mothering Sunday – Importance of Family Bonds

April – Easter – Forgiveness and Life after Death

May – Bank Holidays – Holiday; Times of Refreshment

June – Father's Day – Family and Roots

July/August – Summer Fairs – Community Solidarity

September – School Starts – Changes and New Beginnings

October – Harvest – Providence and Environment

November – Remembrance – Bereavement

December – Christmas – Peace on Earth

Some churches find themselves the centre of attention for weddings because of their venue or their attractive building and it can be a continual struggle to show prospective brides and bridegrooms something of Christian marriage. 'Listening to the Local' research shows that congregations at weddings and baptisms are growing, so how does the local church bring something fresh to these important rites of passage? Commitment is not in vogue today and churches can be perceived as being negative. Couples often quake at the thought of talking to the vicar!

Churches could consider sharing the load as the churches in Barnstaple deanery have done. Ninety couples have been prepared for marriage over the last three years by churches working together across the deanery and, currently, there are plans to put on 'Marriage Refreshment' events. St Mary's, Arnold, near Nottingham have developed their web site to answer many of the questions that wedding enquirers have and after the wedding (or baptism), they have found that couples respond well to an invitation to an Alpha group, or similar, where they can discuss everyday matters of faith. The service can be made more accessible for the congregation too as some churches have done by participating in an online wedding service. Family and friends attending in the flesh can be joined by Internet users who log on to the site to witness the service. At one such wedding in Merseyside, 100 churchgoers were joined by about 250 Internet users and the wedding service clip remained available for up to a month on the host site.[18]

Weddings can remain an important point of connection with parishioners long after the actual event and even after the couple themselves have moved on. St Peter's, Nuthall had a week-long flower festival entitled 'Wedding Memories'. It incorporated a service of thanksgiving for marriage. St Andrew's, Chardstock, went further and held a festival of 'Flowers and Wedding Dresses' to celebrate a century of marriage. The three-day festival captured the interest of many and culminated in a Sunday service. If churches become known as places where family life through marriage and baptism is celebrated and prayerfully supported, many will be encouraged in their spiritual searching and at important stages in their lives to turn to the local church.

Towards a future

I hope that reflecting on our Christian roots and the surprises from research carried out in this area has inspired you to consider where God is pointing your church at the beginning of the twenty-first century. The road map for local churches is very varied and fast-changing but we journey with a God of surprises, a faithful God. If churches and local communities are to have a meaningful conversation together, it is vital that we find *time to listen* to the findings and stories from ongoing research. Many feel that *the* surprising sign of the times is that our Christian roots continue to be valued by many but in ways relevant to twenty-first century Britain. Churches should take heart that what they offer is valued by modern-day Britain. God is at work in our nation in a new way that builds on its inherited faith. The challenge remains that we continue to be an open and listening Church, listening to what God's Spirit is saying through the world to the Church today.

> IF CHURCHES AND LOCAL COMMUNITIES ARE TO HAVE A MEANINGFUL CONVERSATION TOGETHER, IT IS VITAL THAT WE FIND *TIME TO LISTEN* TO THE FINDINGS AND STORIES FROM ONGOING RESEARCH.

Notes

Series Introduction
1. *Evangelism in a Spiritual Age*, Church House Publishing, 2005.
2. Vincent Donovan, *Christianity Rediscovered*, Orbis, 1978, 2003.
3. John Paul II, 'Discourse to the Plenary Assembly of the Pontifical Council for Culture', 18 March 2004, quoted by Trystan Owain Hughes, *Anvil* 22 (1), 2005.
4. J. V. Taylor, *The Go-Between God*, SCM Press, 1973.
5. David Ison (ed.), *The Vicar's Guide*, Church House Publishing, 2005.
6. Clive Marsh, *Christianity in a Post-Atheist Age*, SCM Press, 2002.
7. *Mission-shaped Church*, Church House Publishing, 2005.

Chapter 1 Listening to the Nation
1. Quoted in a research paper by David Hay, 'Why is implicit religion implicit?' October, 2002.
2. David Hay and Kate Hunt, *Understanding the Spirituality of People Who Don't Go to Church*, University of Nottingham, 2000.
3. David Hay, 'Why is implicit religion implicit?' October, 2002.
4. Alan Billings, *Secular Lives, Sacred Hearts*, SPCK, 2004, p. 37.
5. Sources: Gallup polls/Opinion Research Business/ICM.
6. Compiled by Robin Gill in *The Empty Church Revisited*, Ashgate, 2003.
7. Opinion Research Business 2000 for BBC *Soul of Britain* programme series.
8. D. Hay and G. Heald, 'Religion is good for you', New Society, 17 April 1987, quoted in Hay and Hunt, *Understanding the Spirituality of People who Don't Go to Church*, 2000; and Opinion Research Business, 2000.
9. Nina Goswami reporting in the *Daily Telegraph*, 22 August 2005.
10. Private web-based research by the author.
11. Ekklesia web site, 14 September 2005, sponsored by Anvil Trust.
12. G. P. Taylor, *Church of England Newspaper*, 22 July 2005.
13. The *Times*, 16 May 2005.
14. Belief systems reported in R. Gill, *The Empty Church Revisited*, Ashgate, 2003.
15. For BBC *Soul of Britain* programme series, 2000.
16. Populas, 'Beliefs and Morals' national survey for the *Sun*, June 2005.
17. From an article in the *Church of England Newspaper*, 23 July 2004, edited from an address to the City Churches Celebration at St Paul's Cathedral on 14 July 2004.

18. Linda Woodhead writing in the *Church Times*, 31 December 2004.
19. Paul Heelas and Linda Woodhead, *The Spiritual Revolution*, Blackwell, 2005.
20. See *Making Sense of Generation Y*, Church House Publishing, 2006.
21. Ulf Sjodin in Grace Davie, Paul Heelas and Linda Woodhead (eds), *Predicting Religion*, Ashgate, 2003.
22. Populas telephone poll of 1,004 young adults conducted for the *Times* and reported, 14–18 September 2004.
23. For a fuller discussion, see R. Gill in Paul Avis (ed.), *Public Faith*, SPCK, 2003.
24. Quoted by D. Hay in a book review of *The Spirituality Revolution*, *The Tablet*, 21, August 2004.
25. Trystan Owain Hughes, 'Pop Music and the Church's Mission', *Anvil*, 22 (1), 2005.
26. 'Soul tsunami: sink or swim in new millennium culture', Zondervan, Grand Rapids 1999, quoted by Trystan Owain Hughes in 'Pop Music and the Church's Mission'.
27. World Values Survey, London School of Economics, 2005.
28. Gallup Polls Ltd, 2005 reported in the *Guardian*, 15 September 2005.
29. For the BBC *Soul of Britain* programme series.
30. Henley Centre, 'Planning for social change', quoted in The Tomorrow Project, 2000.
31. MORI, 'Whom do we trust?', 27 February 2003.
32. Opinion Research Business, 2000.
33. D. Hay, book review of *The Spirituality Revolution, The Tablet,* 21 August 2004.
34. Alan Billings, *Secular Lives, Sacred Hearts*, SPCK, 2004, p. 104.
35. *Not Easy but Full of Meaning*, Redemptionist Publishing, July 2005.
36. www.cofe.anglican.org/info/statistics
37. Population Trends, Office for National Statistics.
38. Grace Davie, *Europe: The Exceptional Case*, Darton, Longman & Todd, 2002, pp. 12, 52.
39. Davie, *Europe*, p. 5.
40. From composite national poll results by BMRB 2005 and ORB 2005 for Tearfund and the Church of England.
41. Peter Skov-Jacobsen, 'Being church in a secular society', *Crucible*, July–September 2002.

Chapter 2 Listening to the Local
1. Analysis by Revd Rob Merchant and Professor Paul Kingston, University of Wolverhampton.

Christian roots, contemporary spirituality

2. Paper by D. Hay for the British and Irish Association for Mission Studies, September 2000.
3. John Finney, *Finding Faith Today*, Bible Society, 1992.
4. Opinion Research Business national telephone poll, 2005.
5. ORB national poll, 2001.
6. ORB national poll, 2001.
7. Douglas Davies, Charles Watkins and Michael Winter, *Church and Religion in Rural England*, T&T Clark, 1991.
8. David Self, *Church Times*, 19/26 December 2003.
9. Letter to the *Times*, 31 January 2005.
10. MORI, December 2004.
11. Anthony Browne writing in the *Times*, 21 December 2005.
12. Michael Howard in the *Sun*, 9 December 2004.
13. Michael Howard in the *Sun*, 9 December 2004.
14. ORB national telephone polls, 2001, 2003 and 2005.
15. ORB national telephone polls, 2001, 2003 and 2005.
16. The *Times*, 9 June 2005.
17. Grace Davie, University of Exeter, 'From obligation to consumption', paper to Bishops' Day Conference, September 2002.
18. Europe poll reported in the *Times*, 10 March 2005.
19. Paper by G. Heald, 'Soul of Britain at the Millennium', 2001.
20. Population trends, Office for National Statistics, 1 September 2005.
21. As above, 30 September 2005.
22. YouGov national survey, April 2005.
23. 'Marriage is on the rocks as fewer say I do', *Daily Telegraph*, 30 September 2005.
24. Populus national poll for the *Times*, 5 September 2005.
25. 'You and Your Wedding' national survey, February 2005.
26. Maestro UK survey, August 2005.
27. 'Bishops give "Angels" their support', Church of England press release, 19 November 2005.
28. *Church Times*, 3 June 2005, and explored further in Alan Billings, *Secular Lives, Sacred Hearts*, SPCK, 2004.
29. 'Church Life Profile', 2001 survey of churchgoers by Churches Information for Mission.
30. Opinion Research Business national polls, 2001, 2003 and 2005.
31. Alan Billings, *Secular Lives, Sacred Hearts*, SPCK, 2004.

Chapter 3 Listening to the Past

1. Quentin Letts, 'I'm not "devout", that's why I'm an Anglican', *Daily Telegraph* 'Opinion', 3 July 2005.
2. Anne Richards in Paul Avis (ed.), *Public Faith*, SPCK, 2003.
3. Discussed by Martyn Percy in *Public Faith*.
4. A. Hastings, *A History of English Christianity 1920–2000*, SCM Press, 2001, p. 670.
5. Research by Andrew Yip, in Grace Davie, Paul Heelas and Linda Woodhead (eds), *Predicting Religion*, Ashgate, 2003.
6. R. Gill in *Public Faith*.
7. A. Hastings, *A History of English Christianity 1920–2000*, where he dates the overall high point of churchgoing as 1881 and the decline of the Free Churches from 1906.
8. A. Hastings, *A History of English Christianity*.
9. Callum Brown, *Death of Christian Britain*, Routledge, 2001.
10. A. Hastings, *A History of English Christianity*.
11. Review in *The Tablet*, November 2004.
12. D. Voas in *Public Faith*.
13. Bernice Martin in *Public Faith*.
14. From composite national poll results by BMRB 2005 and ORB 2005 for Tearfund and the Church of England.
15. Kate Hunt in *Predicting Religion*.
16. A. Yip in *Predicting Religion*.
17. Grace Davie, *Religion in Britain since 1945*, Blackwell, 1994.
18. Grace Davie, *Europe: The Exceptional Case*, Darton, Longman & Todd, 2002.
19. Davie, *Europe*.
20. Davie, *Europe*.
21. Grace Davie, 'From obligation to consumption', paper to the Bishops' Day Conference, University of Exeter, September 2002.
22. Grace Davie, 'From obligation to consumption'.

Chapter 4 Surprising Signs of the Times

1. See www.24-7prayer.com
2. John Finney, *Emerging Evangelism*, Darton, Longman & Todd, 2004.
3. Melanie Phillips, *Sunday Times*, 2 September 2001, quoted by A. Morgan in *The Wild Gospel*, Monarch Books, 2004.

4. *Church Times*, Regional News, 17 December 2004.
5. I. Tarrant and S. Dakin, *Labyrinths and Prayer Stations*, Grove, 2004.
6. Ian Bradley, 'Coronations will always be a time to rededicate the nation', *Daily Telegraph*, 2 June 2003.
7. *Daily Telegraph*, 18 June 2005.
8. *Church Times*, 27 May 2005.
9. www.pearlsoflife.org
10. Reported in *Bright Futures*, The Children's Society magazine, Autumn 2005.
11. *Church Times*, 21 October 2005.
12. *Church of England Newspaper*, 24/31 December 2004.
13. Opinion Research Business, 2001; national telephone poll for Archbishops' Council et al.
14. Chichester diocesan magazine, Winter 2004/5.
15. Opinion Research Business, 2001.
16. Described by Mark Ireland in *Evangelism in a Spiritual Age*, Church House Publishing, 2005.
17. Quoted in Geoff Pearson, 'Towards the conversion of England', Liverpool diocesan paper, 2004.
18. *Church of England Newspaper*, 10 September 2004.

Acknowledgements

We are grateful to the following for permission to reproduce images in this book:

The Revd Canon John Holmes for the photograph of the prayer station in Wakefield Cathedral (p. 43).

Steve Collins and Matt Cryer for the photograph of the prayer labyrinth in Portsmouth Cathedral (p. 44), copyright © Steve Collins and Matt Cryer.

Pete Dredge for the cartoon that originally appeared in *The Church Times*, 'God is for Life' (p. 48), copyright © Pete Dredge.